All About
Spiders

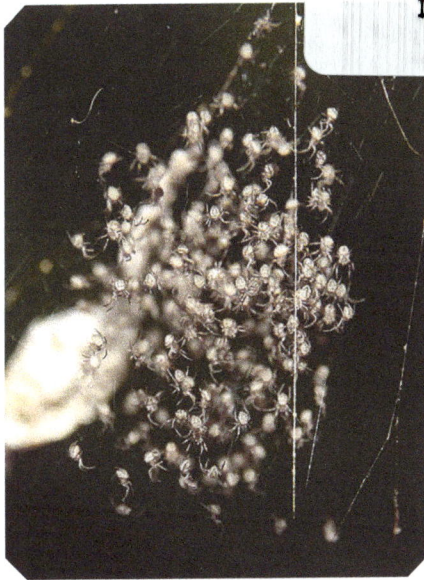

By Christabel Pinto

Library For All Ltd.

Library For All is an Australian not for profit organisation with a mission to make knowledge accessible to all via an innovative digital library solution. Visit us at libraryforall.org

All About Spiders

This edition published 2022

Published by Library For All Ltd
Email: info@libraryforall.org
URL: libraryforall.org

Library For All gratefully acknowledges the contributions of all who made previous editions of this book possible.

This book was made possible by the generous support of Save The Children.

Original illustrations by Public Domain images and Creative Commons Licensed Images

All About Spiders
Pinto, Christabel
ISBN: 978-1-922827-98-2
SKU02704

All About
Spiders

Spiders are everywhere

There are around 40 000 different species of spider that are found on all continents of the world, except Antarctica. Spiders belong to a group of animals called arachnids that have two body segments, eight legs, and no wings or antenna. Other animals that are also part of the arachnid family include scorpions, mites and ticks.

Goliath Birdeater

Big and small

The largest spider in the world by weight is the Goliath birdeater, found in South America. It can weigh over 170 g. In spite of its name, it rarely eats birds! The huntsman spider is the largest spider by leg span, with a leg span that can go up to 30 cm.

patu digua

The *patu digua*, found in Colombia, is considered to be the smallest spider in the world. The male *patu digua* averages 0.37mm in length, which is the size of a small grain of sand.

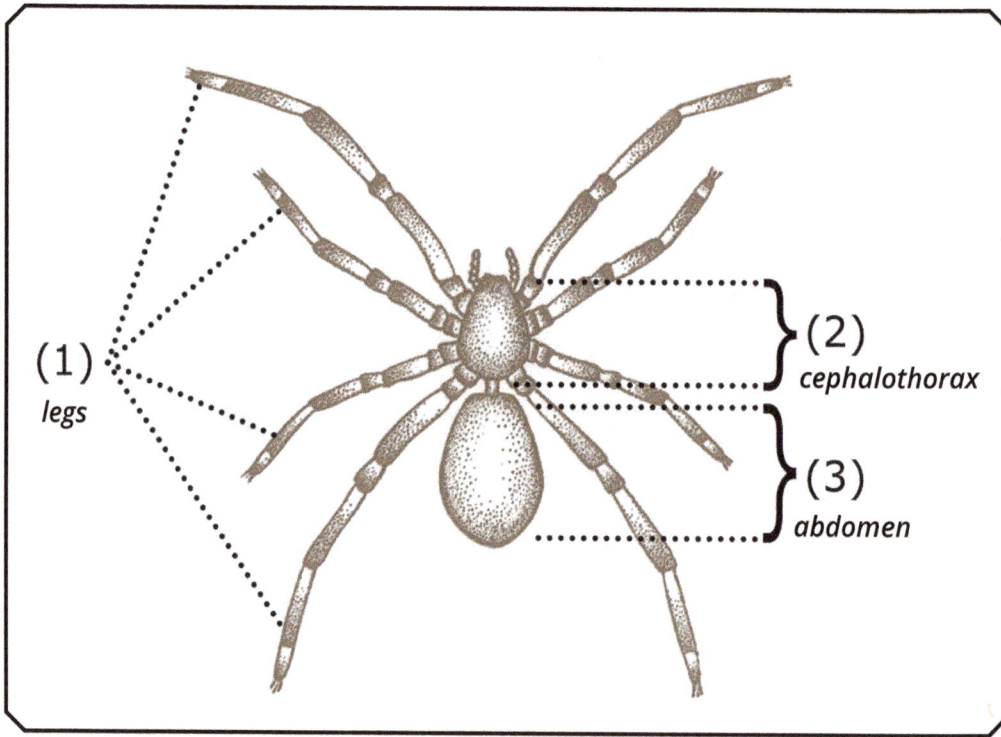

(1)
legs

(2)
cephalothorax

(3)
abdomen

Growing and developing

The front segment of a spider's body is called a cephalothorax, and the second part of the body is called the abdomen. The spider's eyes, mouth fangs, brain, stomach, and venom-producing glands are found on the cephalothorax. The eight legs are also attached to this part of the body. The spider's silk-producing glands, or spinnerets, are found at the end of the abdomen.

How spiders move

When spiders move, there are always four legs on the surface and four legs off the surface. Spiders move using a combination of muscles and hemolymph, which is the fluid in spiders that is like blood in humans. By contracting muscles in the cephalothorax, spiders can increase the hemolymph pressure in a leg to move it.

Producing silk

Spiders are associated with spider webs. But, while all spiders produce silk, not all spiders spin webs. In addition to creating webs, silk can be used for moving, building egg sacks, wrapping prey, and shelter. Different spiders produce different types of silk. Spider silk can be sticky, stretchy or dry.

Food

Spiders are predators, so they catch and eat other animals. Most spiders feed on insects and similar animals, but some spiders can even prey on animals as large as mice, lizards and birds! Can you think of some of the different ways spiders can catch their prey?

Trapping prey in webs

Many spiders build webs to trap insects for food. These spiders don't have good eyesight and use the vibrations of the web strands to locate their trapped prey. When they find their prey, they wrap the prey in silk, turning it around and around, until it is covered before biting it with their teeth.

Hunting for prey

The spiders that do not use webs to trap food, hunt for food in a variety of ways. Some spiders will camouflage by blending in with their surroundings. Then, they will pounce on passing prey. Other spiders have incredible eyesight and can use this ability to first spot their prey from a distance, then chase after them.

Solid food to liquid food

Spiders cannot chew, so they can take in only liquid food. They bite prey with their fangs and insert venom that poisons the prey. Spiders inject digestive juices into their prey that turns the inside of the prey into a liquid that they can digest.

Reproduction

Female spiders are often larger than males. Mating can be dangerous for males because the female might think the male is prey! Males send gentle vibrations through a web that would be different from the vibrations of trapped prey, or males will do a dance to attract the female. A male nursery spider will present the female with a gift of an insect to satisfy her hunger so that she will not eat him!

Baby spiders

Spiders can lay between two and 1000 eggs, depending on the species. Most females will protect the eggs by wrapping them in silk and then hanging them in a silk egg sac, which she will then guard until the baby spiders are born. After the babies hatch, they will often stay inside the sac to finish developing.

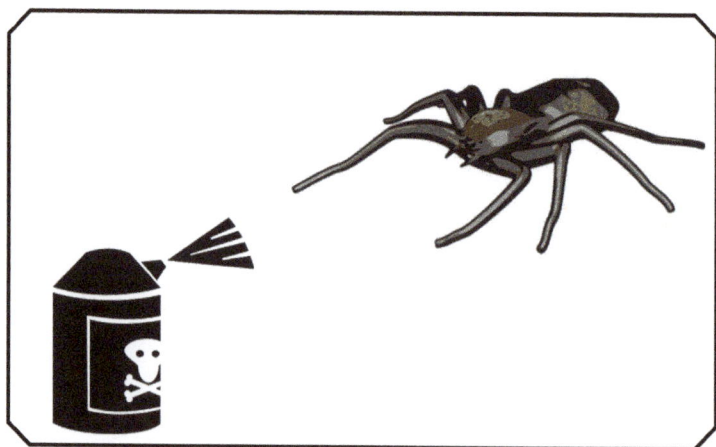

Threats to spiders

Spiders can be the prey of larger animals, such as lizards, birds, toads and monkeys. The worst predator of the spider is the spider wasp, which can paralyse a spider by stinging it. People also harm spiders when using insecticides or insect-killing chemicals.

Fun facts about spiders

- The strongest material in the world is considered to be the silk that spiders create.
- Most spiders have eight eyes, but some have fewer.
- Spiders are near-sighted, which means they cannot see objects that are far away.

- When spiders grow, they molt. This means that they shed their skin and grow a new skin to take its place.
- Spiders recycle their silk. They eat up old silk that is no longer useful.
- 'Arachnophobia' is a fear of spiders.
- Most spiders are harmless to humans. Even if they inject venom into humans, death by a spider bite is very rare!

Glossary

Abdomen: the back part of the spider

Arachnids: a group of animals that have two body segments, eight legs, and no wings or antenna

Cephalothorax: the front part of the spider, which the legs are attached to

Digestive juices: fluids that animals produce, which help them break down food

Hemolymph: the circulating fluid in spiders that is like the blood in humans

Predators: animals that eat other animals

Prey: an animal hunted or seized for food

Spinnerets: silk-producing glands that are found at the end of the abdomen

Venom: a poison that is secreted by animals by biting or stinging their prey

You can use these questions to talk about this book with your family, friends and teachers.

What did you learn from this book?

Describe this book in one word. Funny? Scary? Colourful? Interesting?

How did this book make you feel when you finished reading it?

What was your favourite part of this book?

download our reader app
getlibraryforall.org

About the contributors

Library For All works with authors and illustrators from around the world to develop diverse, relevant, high quality stories for young readers. Visit libraryforall.org for the latest news on writers' workshop events, submission guidelines and other creative opportunities.

Did you enjoy this book?

We have hundreds more expertly curated original stories to choose from.

We work in partnership with authors, educators, cultural advisors, governments and NGOs to bring the joy of reading to children everywhere.

Did you know?

We create global impact in these fields by embracing the United Nations Sustainable Development Goals.

libraryforall.org

www.ingramcontent.com/pod-product-compliance
Lightning Source LLC
Chambersburg PA
CBHW040313050426
42452CB00018B/2822